Word and Table

Supplemental Worship Resources 3

Word and Table

A Basic Pattern of Sunday Worship for United Methodists with Introduction and Commentary

Revised Edition 1980

Abingdon
Nashville

WORD AND TABLE

A Basic Pattern of Sunday Worship for United Methodists

Revised Edition 1980

6th Printing

Copyright © 1976 and 1980 by Abingdon

ISBN 0-687-46127-8

Manufactured by the Parthenon Press at Nashville, Tennessee. United States of America.

CONTENTS

I.
Pattern and Orders of Service

A Basic Pattern of Worship

ENTRANCE AND PRAISE

The people come together in the Lord's name. There may be greetings, music and song, prayer and praise.

PROCLAMATION AND PRAISE

The Scriptures are opened to the people through readings, preaching, witnessing, music, or other arts and media. Interspersed may be psalms, anthems, or hymns.

RESPONSES AND OFFERINGS

Responses to God's Word include acts of commitment and faith with offerings of concerns, prayers, gifts, and service for the world and for one another.

THE HOLY MEAL

The actions of Jesus in the upper room are reenacted:
taking the bread and cup,
giving thanks over the bread and cup,
breaking the bread, and
giving the bread and cup.

SENDING FORTH

The people are sent into the world with the Lord's blessing.

An Order of Sunday Worship

Gathering
Greeting
Hymn of Praise
Opening Prayer(s)
[Act of Praise]
[Prayer for Illumination]
Scripture Lection
[Psalm or Anthem]
[Scripture Lection]
Hymn or Song
Gospel Lection
Sermon
Response to the Word
Concerns and Prayers
The Peace
Offering

or

Non-Communion Days

Prayer of Thanksgiving
Lord's Prayer

Communion Days

Taking the Bread and Cup
Great Thanksgiving
Breaking the Bread
Giving the Bread and Cup

Hymn or Song
Dismissal with Blessing
Going Forth

The bread and wine are brought to the Lord's Table or are uncovered, if already in place. The minister makes any necessary preparation of the elements and then prays the Great Thanksgiving according to the following pattern:

The Lord be with you.
And also with you.
Lift up your hearts.
We lift them to the Lord.
Let us give thanks to the Lord our God.
It is right to give him thanks and praise.

The minister gives thanks appropriate to the occasion, remembering God's acts of salvation, and concludes:
Therefore, with your people in all ages
and the whole company of heaven,
we join in the song of unending praise, saying:

Holy, holy, holy Lord, God of power and might,
heaven and earth are full of your glory.
Hosanna in the highest.
Blessed is he who comes in the name of the Lord.
Hosanna in the highest.

The minister continues the thanksgiving, recalls the institution of the Lord's Supper, prays that we may be joined with Christ's offering for us, invokes the power of the Holy Spirit, and praises the Trinity, concluding:
All glory and honor is yours, Almighty God (*Father*)
now and for ever.
Amen.

LORD'S PRAYER

The Minister breaks the bread.

The bread and wine are given to the people with these or other words being exchanged:

The body of Christ, given for you. **Amen.**
The blood of Christ, given for you. **Amen.**

The congregation sings hymns.

9

An Order with the Sick or Shut-in

Greeting

Reading(s) from Scripture

Comment on Scripture

Prayer

Taking the Bread and Cup

The Great Thanksgiving

Breaking the Bread

Giving the Bread and Cup

Prayer and Blessing

Sign of Peace

There should be whatever participation is possible by the person(s) receiving Communion. Sometimes this may be simply gestures and expression. Where possible it should include, with the readings from Scripture, the recitation of a psalm or other Scripture or the recitation or singing of a hymn.

The sharing of the person's concerns and prayer requests could take place before the prayer or whenever the person felt ready.

The Calendar

II.
Introduction

United Methodists, along with many other traditions within the Christian family of faith, are in the midst of the reform and renewal of worship. This is part of the ongoing struggle to be a more faithful and vital church. The reform and renewal of our Sunday worship is not simply a matter of producing a new liturgy and new forms and materials for worship; it is nothing less than the recovery of Christ in the life of the church and its mission in the world.

United Methodists received *The Sacrament of the Lord's Supper: An Alternate Text 1972* (SWR1) with considerable enthusiasm, and similar success for its successor "A Sunday Service" in *We Gather Together* (SWR 10), 1980, seems assured. This favorable reception indicates increasing recognition that both the proclamation of the Word and the celebration of the Lord's Supper form the heart of our congregational worship. The structure and language of these texts represent a thoroughgoing reform of United Methodist worship practices. This book builds upon that reform and proposes a basic pattern from which variety of developing orders can emerge. Let us examine briefly some new features of this pattern, its biblical and historical roots, its theology, and some key pastoral and practical issues.

New Features of This Pattern

This basic pattern and related orders of worship seek to incorporate the insights that have emerged during a period of great sharing among many Christian traditions. We are here moving beyond a simple revision of inherited patterns and Reformation liturgies to a much broader, more inclusive heritage from the early church as well. In this sense it is more richly historical than either John Wesley's Sunday Service for Methodists in North America (1784), and the Anglican Prayer Book service of 1549 upon which the present order in *The Book of Worship* (1965) is based, or the various Evangelical and United Brethren orders. It also allows for the development of an evangelical style of worship because of its adaptability and its reflection of early Christian patterns.

The structure and unfolding rhythm of the alternate service's basic pattern clearly show the influence of some of the earliest liturgies in the Christian community. The two-fold division of the liturgy of the Word and the liturgy of the Thanksgiving Meal reflects early practices. There is a new emphasis upon thanksgiving and praise, upon the reading and proclamation of Scripture, and upon the role of the Holy Spirit in the worship of God's people. In one sense, then, this basic pattern of worship is historically older than most of our recent patterns. The restoration of the unified liturgy of the early churches, consisting of the reading of Scripture and proclamation, congregational prayer, praise and response, and the sacramental sign-actions of bread and wine, brings forth new theological understandings. Word and sacrament thus complete and fulfill one another: this pattern of worship seeks to recover that profound truth for the contemporary life of The United Methodist Church.

Many persons will ask, "Why does the full order of worship include both the service of the Word and the celebration of the Sacrament?" Most United Methodists have been accustomed to a preaching service as the regular pattern for Sunday worship. The Lord's Supper, or Holy Communion, has often been regarded as an occasional service, celebrated quarterly or at best monthly. Many regard the Sacrament as something added on to the "regular" service. *The Book of Worship* (1965) and former E.U.B. rites in the *Book of Ritual* (1959) include full services of preaching and sacrament, but these have not been widely regarded as the usual pattern in practice. Recent years have seen a growing tendency toward a monthly celebration of the Lord's Supper in many churches. As a general rule, however, the United Methodist Church is not accustomed to the idea of a service of preaching and sacrament as normal for every Lord's Day.

Two points must be emphasized. First, the celebration of the Thanksgiving Meal is a *way of doing,* not only a ritual order of words. Worship is far more than the right words in the right order, and much more than something "preached." Increasing numbers of Christians understand and desire worship to be a corporate action of the gathered community. The basic pattern presented here may enable us to experience more clearly this corporate enactment of the story and the mystery of the Christian faith. The action character of worship is especially evident in the sacraments of Baptism and the Lord's Supper. The sacraments are *eventful* and involve the body and all our senses, and not merely the hearing of words recited.

Second, whether or not the service on a given Sunday includes the Lord's Supper, it is important that we recover the basic shape and intent of the full order. The presence of Christ is known, by the aid of the Spirit, in the assembly gathered in his name, in Scripture and proclamation, prayer and praise. The full experience of the Word is completed in the celebration of the Meal. By this we recognize that Christ is present to his people in many ways. This basic pattern and alternate orders of worship are

14

intended as vehicles for enabling the congregation to experience Christ more fully in the worshiping assembly.

Biblical and Historical Roots

The biblical and historical roots for this pattern and the content of these services are clear and compelling. The first page of the service has its origins in the synagogue with which Jesus and the early church were familiar. (See Luke 4:14 ff. and Acts 13:13 ff.) This is sometimes called the *synaxis*, or "gathering." The basic elements are simple: a greeting in the Lord's name, praise, opening prayers, the reading and hearing of the Scriptures interspersed with psalms, teaching and proclamation, affirmations and corporate prayers. Essentially, this is a slightly amplified version of the synagogue pattern. These basic elements may be simplified or elaborated without destroying the rhythm and movement of the service.

Following the actual gathering in the Lord's name, the synaxis focuses primarily upon Scripture and proclamation in the context of prayer and praise. In his *First Apology* (c. A.D. 155), Justin Martyr writes:

And on the day called Sunday there is a meeting in one place of those who live in cities or the country, and the memoirs of the apostles or the writings of the prophets are read as long as time permits. When the reader has finished, the presider (president) in a discourse urges and invites (us) to the imitation of these noble things. Then we all stand up and offer prayers (chapter 67).

The singing of psalms and spiritual songs (Col. 3:16) along with responsive witness was undoubtedly part of this early service of the Word and Spirit. Thereafter followed the second main section of the liturgy, as Justin indicates:

15

And, as said before, when we have finished the prayer, bread is brought, and wine with water, and the president similarly sends up prayers and thanksgivings to the best of his ability, and the congregation assents, saying the Amen; the distribution and reception of the consecrated (elements) by each one takes place and they are sent to the absent by deacons.*

The second main part of the service focuses upon the sacramental action of the Meal. The Lord's Supper, or Thanksgiving Meal, enacts the supper of Jesus with his disciples in the context of Passover, the post-resurrection meals with the disciples (Luke 24; John 21), and the apostolic gatherings for the breaking of bread described in Acts 2. The enacted rite with bread and wine has been called by various Christian traditions the Lord's Supper, the Holy Communion, the Lord's Memorial, the Holy Supper, the Eucharist, the Mass, or the Divine Liturgy. The most fundamental meaning and character of the meal is "eucharistic" (from the New Testament Greek word meaning "thanksgiving"). Yet it also joins the mystery of Christ's passion and death with the resurrection appearances and his continuing presence in the life of his people. Thus, "Do this in remembrance of me" is forever fused with the experienced death and resurrection of Jesus Christ in the faithful gathering of the baptized. Here we celebrate and practice the story and reality of our redemption in Christ. Here we are given gifts, and we in turn offer our sacrifice of praise and thanksgiving and ourselves to God.

Despite the separate origins of these two principal parts of the service, they are knit together into one unified liturgy quite early in the church's life, perhaps even from New Testament times (Acts 20) and certainly from the second

*We may note this early reference to the practice of serving the sick and shut-in the bread and wine consecrated in the celebration of the gathered community. In our suggested pattern for Communion with the sick or shut-in, we may indeed find the recovery of this ancient practice, both theologically and pastorally, a powerful extension of corporate worship.

century on. In the basic shape of our alternate order we discern the remarkable simplicity of the four-fold action of the Lord's Supper: take bread and wine; give thanks over them by blessing God and reciting the story of creation and redemption, focusing upon the incarnation, ministry, death, and resurrection-ascension of Jesus; break the bread; and finally, give and receive the bread and cup. (See I Cor. 11:23 ff, Matt. 26:26 ff, Mark 14:17 ff, and Luke 22:14 ff.)

In the following centuries a great variety of eleboration developed and eventually obscured the simple actions. Gradually the reality of a corporate celebration and sharing was lost to the priestly performance of the rite on behalf of the worshipers. The Reformers and, to a certain extent, the Catholic Counter-Reformers, attempted to correct these basic problems, along with the other abuses of Word and Sacrament. These new United Methodist orders, along with nearly every other recent reformed eucharistic service in the major Christian traditions, may be regarded as a further step toward recovery and revitalization of the church's most central act of worship. Thus, a primary aim in this pattern is to uncover and make powerful the movement and simple actions of the services of the early church and to restore the vital and active role of the people at worship.

The synagogue/upper-room pattern is more clearly discerned in our new order than in previous United Methodist orders. The essential four-fold shape of the sacramental action itself is clear: (1) the bringing and preparing of the bread and wine (and all the gifts of earth); (2) the Great Thanksgiving with its recalling of Christ's saving work, its presenting of gifts, its prayer that the Spirit may enliven us and the giving of the bread and cup; (3) the breaking of the bread and taking of the cup, using the words of Paul to proclaim our unity in the body of Christ; and (4) the profound action of sharing the elements in

17

corporate communion in, with, and through Jesus Christ. The service concludes with praise and with the sending forth to love and serve God and the neighbor. Thus, the whole service points the worshipers toward a joyful life and faithful mission in the world.

While this basic pattern is a departure from our recent traditions, it is actually a return to the ancient and now emerging stream of Christian practice. With this pattern we may now share fundamentally the same basic pattern of worship with other denominations. This does not automatically mean that we share the same theology or doctrinal convictions about the sacraments, or that we make the same emphases as do other Christian traditions. It does mean, however, that if we come to celebrate Word and the sacraments according to the shape and possibility of the alternate service, we all have much more in common with other Christians across denominational lines. We may move a step toward the realization of Christ's prayer "that they may all be one" (John 17). In belonging to him, we may worship with the faithful "at all times and in all places."

New Theological Understandings

These orders of service and the accompanying texts and prayers accent new theological understandings, some of which have already been suggested. Let us consider several key theological emphases to be discovered in the study and use of these materials.

First, there is a new accent upon joyful praise and thanksgiving. The service of the Lord's Supper joins sacrifice (Heb. 13:15-16) with a clearer note of thanksgiving and celebration of what God has done in Christ. We present ourselves (Rom. 12:1) in union with the universal work of Christ and all the gifts God has given us to offer. The very form of the thanksgiving prayers expresses this

18

theological understanding. They are shaped by the Hebrew notion of *berakah*: to bless God, and to bless or consecrate something by giving thanks to God for it. Thus, to do the Eucharist (to give thanks, to eucharistize—I Cor. 10:16-17) is to respond to our creation, to our redemption, and to the promise of the Kingdom by offering our "sacrifice of praise and thanksgiving."

Second, there is a clearer theological emphasis upon the centrality of Scripture and proclamation. The reading, singing, and hearing of Scripture are necessary to the proclamation of the Word in the midst of the assembly. The sermon is part of the proclaiming and hearing of the Scriptures, thus emphasizing preaching as a contemporary witness to the Word. The placement of the sermon toward the central part of the service provides a fuller context for congregational response to the Word. These orders allow for more congregational participation in Scripture, read and proclaimed. Indeed, this demonstrates the very root meaning of *liturgy:* the "work of the people."

Third, a more prominent place is given to remembrance as a vivid presentation of the past which directs us to our future in God's kingdom. We remember and proclaim the history of God's creating, sustaining, and redeeming work in Israel and the church and the whole world. When we "remember" Jesus Christ, we do his *anamnesis* (the New Testament word usually translated "remembrance"); that is, we recall and reappropriate him in the present so that we are caught up into his very being and are continuing the redemptive history of God-with-us. Thus, in our corporate memory, recited and proclaimed, we are given identity in Christ and the hope of his future kingdom of which we have a foretaste in the meal.

Fourth, a more prominent place is given to the Holy Spirit in worship. The living experience of encounter and fellowship with God in proclamation and praise is accented especially in the prayer for illumination and in the invoking of the Spirit on the people and the gifts. The Sacrament of the Lord's Supper is to be marked by an awareness of the Spirit's power and the presence of Jesus Christ in the entire action of Word and Meal. Moreover, the Spirit is seen in the various ministries of the people at prayer and in their work in the world, which is here joined with the work of Christ. Thus a distinctive, though not exclusive, note is sounded in testimony to grace and to experienced life in the Spirit in both Word and Sacrament.

Fifth, the recovery of congregational prayer and praise is at the heart of the people's participation in worship. The prayers of the people for the church and for the world are an expression of the priesthood of all believers. In these services a new awareness of prayer as sacramental activity may be brought to life. The people's prayers and praise are indeed the "work of the people of God," thus emphasizing a theology of the laity in worship.

Finally, as expressed in these orders, Christian worship is to be celebrated and experienced in light of the promise of the kingdom of God yet to be fully revealed. We are to love, serve, and worship God as his people "between the times" of God's redemptive acts in history and his coming in final victory at the end of history. This idea is emphasized in the people's acclamations in the thanksgiving prayer: "Christ has died, Christ is risen, Christ will come again." Also present is the conviction that our worship through time, including the seasons of the year, can express the richness of this eschatological hope and understanding. This joyful foretaste is truly for all seasons.

In suggesting that the full service of Word and Lord's Supper become the norm, we express a deeper theological understanding of celebration. In the Sacrament of Word and Meal we are given a history more powerful than mere "remembered events" and a future far greater than natural expectation. These are the great gifts of God, who in worship makes us present to one another and himself present to us.

Practical Problems

More frequent celebrations of the Lord's Supper bring a number of practical problems that must be handled with pastoral sensitivity. In many churches attendance now goes down on Communion Sundays, and the thought of increasing the frequency of its celebration is a major stumbling block. Even where attendance is stable or rises on Communion Sundays, there still may be resistance to celebrating it more often.

One problem concerns the length of the service. Under the older pattern and customary manner of worship on Communion Sundays, the service often seems uncomfortably long. In some local churches people are relaxed about the time and duration of worship, but in others there is often serious objection to extending the service beyond the length of an hour. Therefore the time scheme of the entire service and its essential parts must be considered together.

We may find help in learning from other traditions which celebrate both the Word and the Lord's Supper more frequently, even weekly. Often the full service may take no more time than many United Methodist preaching services without Communion. Where time is a problem, the service may move quickly to the reading and preaching of the Word. Preaching may gain strength by being shortened and sharply focused. Most congregations take longer in giving and receiving the communion elements than is necessary. There is a variety of ways to give and receive the bread and cup, and each congregation will need to find what is for them the best mode of communing. Specific suggestions can be found on pages 40 ff. of the commentary which follows.

Another problem is that of maintaining sufficient variety through the year. One reason for this has been the lack of options that has characterized the text of our traditional ritual. That ritual, furthermore, tends to reinforce the idea

21

of Communion as necessarily solemn and penitential in tone—a tone that is appropriate at some times but not others. The 1972 and 1980 services mark improvement in several respects and, when celebrated with options reflecting the various seasons of the Christian year, will address this problem more effectively. A chief consideration in the development of services based on the orders in this book should be an appropriate balance between what is varied and what is unchanging.

Still another problem is the need for a long-term re-education in the basic theology of the Lord's Supper. Three major misunderstandings call for correction. Some have misunderstood Paul's point in I Corinthians 11:17-32, thinking that one must have earned the right to receive Communion by being "worthy." On the other hand, many regard the Lord's Supper as an imitation of a sorrowful Last Supper in which we continually rehearse our unworthiness. Still others participate in the body of Christ too casually (I Cor. 11:29), thus failing to discern the holiness of Christ's self-giving and of our relationships with one another. The Lord's Supper should be understood and experienced as the celebration of the total saving work of Christ, who has passed through suffering and death to resurrection, thereby redeeming his people.

A closely related problem is the idea that Communion is an occasional service of renewal and rededication that should not be celebrated too often for fear of losing its impact. This idea is often expressed in those churches where the only occasions for Communion may be at New Year's, Maundy Thursday, World Communion Sunday, and during a retreat, mission, or summer camp. While Communion on such occasions is surely appropriate, we deprive ourselves if we limit it to these times. Communion is an ongoing nourishment of our life and growth in Christ.

There is, to be sure, the need for special occasions of rededication and renewal of our covenant with God. "A

22

Service of Baptism, Confirmation, and Renewal" (*We Gather Together,* pp. 13-17) used as a periodic renewal service, provides for this need. The study and use of such a renewal service holds great promise for understanding the need for the regular gathering to celebrate the full service of Word and Supper. Thus it is that we continually renew our life in Christ, and only in this way can the full significance of living out our baptism be made clear.

An Extraordinary Opportunity

With "A Sunday Service" (*We Gather Together,* pp. 5-11), and this booklet, we have an extraordinary opportunity to recover what John Wesley advocated and practiced: "constant Communion." But with these resources we can also move toward life as the people of God in a new ecumenical spirit, seeking to be truly evangelical, reformed, and catholic, while yet treasuring our distinctive United Methodist emphases. The whole of our faith is focused upon the proclaiming of the good news in Christ, the sharing his meal with those having been incorporated into his death and resurrection through the water and Spirit in Christian baptism, and the living out of that life in gratitude and service. Thus, renewal of our worship is deeply interwoven with renewal of church discipline and with the spiritual renewal of the life of Christ in our midst.

We express the hope that the full service of Word and Sacrament will eventually become normative for United Methodist worship on the Lord's Day. Whether or not the Lord's Supper is celebrated on a given Sunday, ministers and congregations should seek to deepen their understanding of the relation of gathering, proclaiming, and responding, to the mystery of our communion with the living Christ and with one another as members of his body. In this way we have the promise of the unfathomable riches of Christ at the heart of our common worship.

23

III.
Commentary

Gathering

What are people doing as the congregation gathers for worship? Several different patterns are found in United Methodist congregations. Among these are: (1) conversation, informal greetings, and fellowship; (2) quiet meditation and private prayer, commonly with an organ or instrumental prelude; (3) a period of informal singing; (4) sharing of announcements, welcoming, and concerns; and (5) rehearsal of music and other acts of worship which are new to the people. Sometimes there is a combination of the above patterns, as when (1) is encouraged before the prelude begins or before persons have entered the place of worship, and (2) is encouraged thereafter, with (3), (4), or (5) perhaps following the prelude. Sometimes it is possible to relate the music of the prelude to the theme or the music of the service as a whole, and this can be especially effective in focusing the people's attention.

None of these patterns in itself is more valid than another, but one pattern or combination may be far more appropriate than another, depending upon the congregation, the specific circumstances of the day, and the nature of the service itself. Some congregations find it best to vary their pattern of gathering; others find one pattern that is best for them all the time.

Greeting

The greeting may be a Scripture sentence or an exchange between leader and people. It should be acknowledged in these opening words that the congregation is gathered in the Lord's name and that he calls and constitutes our worship. For this reason it is fitting that these opening words lead immediately to a hymn, song, or prayer addressed directly to God.

Hymn of Praise

The opening hymn or song is most appropriately corporate praise to God, theologically related to the principal attributes of God which call forth gratitude and praise. The music and the text should both be strong.

Where the architecture of the worship space or the occasion calls for an entrance of choir and worship leaders, this processional hymn or entrance song should come *before* the greeting, allowing the opening words to be spoken facing the people rather than from behind them. An entrance song may be restrained and formal, or it may be festive and spontaneous, depending upon the context. It is the joyous movement of musicians and leaders toward the focus of gathered attentiveness to God. Processions may include a cross, Bible, banners, posters, and candles.

Some congregations may wish to have the entire community move into place during an entrance song, perhaps following preparatory prayers or other activities elsewhere. This will depend in part upon the size of the congregation and the design of the building.

In any event, it is appropriate to stand during the singing of this hymn or song.

Opening Prayer(s)

Prayer at the opening of worship, together with singing addressed to God, establishes that our worship is a communion with the living God as well as with one another. It includes recognition of who we are before God by centering upon the nature and gifts of God.

A great variety of types and forms of opening prayer is possible, provided that we know what the point of our prayer-action is and how it works with other parts of the service. An opening prayer should intensify the awareness of the congregation of its activity, while moving toward the acts of worship which follow. Two major patterns are suggested.

1) A sequence of (a) call to confession, (b) prayer of confession, (c) silence, and (d) declaration of pardon—which may be a dialogue form of mutual pardon and assurance or prayer for pardon. The prayer of confession and declaration of pardon belong together; neither should be used without the other.

2) A collect, or opening prayer, that addresses God in the light of the theme of the day (cf. examples in *Seasons of the Gospel*, SWR 6). It may be prayed in unison or led by one person. It may be preceded or followed by silence. The prayer may be spontaneous, but it should be brief and to the point.

This service is more flexible with regard to confession than some orders of worship have been in the past. A confessional sequence like (1) is particularly recommended for use during Lent, on appropriate Sundays in Advent, and during other times of penitence in the life of a congregation or community. Some congregations use this sequence every Sunday. There is a danger, however, that the use of this confession sequence can become automatic or routine. It is by no means necessary that it be used every Sunday, particularly since the notes of confession and pardon are often present in the prayers of the day and in other acts of worship. When it is used, self-examination should be encouraged as preparation before coming to the service. The recovery of spiritual discipline outside the standard time for worship is to be sought after, so that our common worship does not always bear the burden of introspection and penitential moods, especially during the celebration of the Lord's Supper.

On occasions, confession/pardon may make more sense following the sermon, as noted below in this commentary.

There is no single correct posture for the congregation during prayer. The biblical tradition of standing to pray is always appropriate, especially when the people have been standing for praise immediately before, and perhaps after, the prayer. Kneeling for prayer is also appropriate, especially in confession. Praying seated and bowed is acceptable, especially if the alternatives are for persons to be kept standing or kneeling for an uncomfortable length of time.

[*Act of Praise*]

This act, like others set in brackets, can be omitted without detracting from the integrity of the order of worship; but it is an excellent opportunity for praising God, to whom we have just prayed. There are several possibilities.

1) This is the point in the service where choirs most commonly sing, though they may also sing between the lessons or at the time of the offering. Sometimes the character of the music may suggest its placement in the order of worship. A musical text praising God for his pardoning mercy, for instance, could most fittingly be sung

following confession and pardon. On the other hand, a general anthem of praise is usually appropriate at any of these points in the service. Since it is best, when possible, to include the whole congregation in any act of worship, there is a growing movement toward the use of musical forms in which the whole congregation has a familiar or easily learned part to sing.

2) The most traditional acts of praise at this point in the service are the ancient and biblical acts of praise which are printed in a new and ecumenical translation in this booklet. Older translations of these and other ancient acts of praise, some of them set to music, are found in *The Book of Hymns*. If possible, these should be sung by the whole congregation. "Lord, have mercy" (*Kyrie*) need not be considered penitential; it may be said or sung as an acclamation. "Glory to God in the highest" (*Gloria in Excelsis*) is especially rich in praise. These two have been sung in some churches every Sunday for many centuries; and while we are not recommending them for use every Sunday, we hope the congregations will be familiar with them.

3) A hymn, hymn stanza, chorus, or doxology may be sung. See under "Doxologies" in *The Book of Hymns* (851). Here hymns based on the Psalms are especially appropriate.

4) This is also an appropriate place in the service for a spoken litany of praise especially composed or selected for the occasion.

[*Prayer for Illumination*]

This prayer asks for the Spirit's guidance in our hearing and understanding. Its focus is upon the work of the Holy Spirit in enabling the people to listen for the Word of God and the reader and the preacher to proclaim the Word. In many churches this prayer is prayed in unison by the congregation or led by a lay person. If the preceding act of praise has been omitted, prayer for illumination can be included in the opening prayers. In some instances the prayer of the day will serve as a prayer for illumination.

This prayer serves as a bridge between the initial section of the service and the proclamation of the Word. The initial section of our worship should be uncluttered and should serve to bring us to full, conscious participation. It should not be unduly dramatic, nor should it be a prolonged series of devotional exercises. It should be one focused gesture of the congregation, heading directly toward the reading, proclaiming, and hearing of the Word of God.

Proclamation and Praise

The whole section of the service from the first lection through the sermon should be regarded as a coherent movement. From the earliest times, the Scripture lections, read and proclaimed, have constituted the heart of the teaching and preaching of the church. This pattern of worship is designed to reassert the primacy of Scripture and the direct relation of the Scripture to preaching or other forms of interpretation. United Methodist worship has often failed to provide adequate coverage of the Bible. Often there has been only one lection, with little or no attention being given to the systematic presentation of the Bible over a period of time.

The historic practice of following a lectionary, or regular cycle of Scripture lessons, has much to commend it. The three-year ecumenical lectionary in *Seasons of the Gospel* is suggested for the serious consideration of United Methodists. It includes for each Sunday a first lection (usually from the Old Testament), a second lection (usually from some part of the New Testament other than the four Gospels), and a lesson from the Gospels. The sequence of lessons in this lectionary has its own coherence. When it is not followed, care should be taken to give such coherence to the lections.

When Scripture is read, the visual impact as well as the sound is important. Reading the lessons from a large pulpit Bible that all the people can see shows forcefully the importance of Scripture in worship. In some congregations the Bible is brought in as part of the opening procession, placed on the pulpit, and opened at the beginning of the proclamation of the Word. When this Bible remains open in front of the preacher during the sermon, it symbolizes visually that the sermon comes from the Scriptures.

Special thought should be given to the words used to introduce and close the reading of Scripture. Introductory comments explaining the setting of the Scripture lection are often appropriate, but they should be brief and to the point. Lections may be immediately preceded by such words as: "Hear the Word of God in a reading from _____." In closing, the reader might say: "This is the Word of the Lord," or simply, "Amen," after which the people might say, "Amen."

Scripture can be presented in many other ways. The congregation may follow the reading silently in their own Bibles, read the lection or alternate verses in unison, or repeat key phrases after the reader. Stories or parables may be dramatized or danced, live or on film. There may be visual or instrumental accompaniment.

The use between Scripture lections of appropriate psalms or of hymns or anthems related to the Scripture texts is derived from ancient Jewish and Christian practice. These give the whole congregation a more active part in the proclamation of the Word. The Psalms are also part of the Word of God, especially since they are a form of sung prayer and praise as well. In this use, the Psalms are not properly Old Testament lections but are responses to the first lection. When a psalm is used as an act of praise, it is appropriate for the congregation to stand and for the psalm to be followed by the saying or singing of the "Glory to the Father" (*Gloria Patri*). Appropriate choral music, especially if based on a psalm, may be used in place of a psalm. A hymn or song may serve as a connecting link between lections. Psalms and hymns from *The Book of Hymns* that are related to the theme and lections for each Sunday of the Christian Year are suggested with the lectionary in this booklet. Here the "Index of Scripture References of Hymns" in *The Book of Hymns* (847) is a helpful resource.

The full and ancient pattern of three lections, interspersed with psalter and singing, is recommended; but this can be shortened to lection, hymn or song, and lection without detracting from the integrity of the service. If only two lections are used regularly, care should be taken to present the whole biblical message over a period of time.

The reading and preaching of the Bible are so closely linked that nothing ought to come between them. To emphasize this unity, the ancient and ecumenical practice of placing the sermon immediately following the last lection is strongly recommended. Some ministers pray immediately before preaching, but if one takes seriously the unity of reading and preaching in the proclamation of the Word, it would seem more fitting to invoke God's help in the prayer for illumination before the proclamation and praise section of the service, as was suggested above.

The placement of the sermon at this point in the service is in keeping with its central importance. The omission of preaching on Communion Sundays violates the unity of Word and Sacrament; however it is not necessary to preach on the subject of the Lord's Supper every time we celebrate it.

The sermon is often strengthened rather than weakened if it is conceived in flexible and imaginative terms. A short sermon is often more effective than a long one and should

31

not be called a sermonette or meditation. Dialogue, dramatization, audiovisual accompaniment, use of objects, and active congregational participation are among the many possibilities during the sermon. Lay speaking, drama (live or on film), or a musical presentation which proclaims the Word can on occasion constitute the sermon.

Many churches are using readings from contemporary sources or from older nonbiblical literature. Where these assist in proclaiming the Word, they can be most appropriate. They can be incorporated into the sermon, as poetry and literary quotations traditionally have been, or they can stand by themselves. They should *not*, however, be substituted for the Scripture lections, but should supplement them.

Response to the Word

Here begins the third major section of the service. As the proclamation and praise is preceded by the gathering of the church, so it should be followed by a response. The order of worship here presented is an attempt to strengthen this vital section of the service, which is neglected in many congregations.

The term "response to the Word," though it will be new to many, has a rich variety of meaning and possibilities. It is to be understood here as indicating a specific occasion for decision, witness, or reflection in accord with the content of the proclamation. Immediately following the sermon, any one or more of the following actions are appropriate:

1) Invitation to Christin discipleship. This may be accompanied by a hymn or song. It may be a specific invitation for commitment to Christ and his church. It may lead into any of the responses to the Word listed below, to specific courses of action, or into the concerns and prayers of the church.

2) Silent reflection and spoken expressions from the congregation. These may take various forms. There may be a period of corporate silence, broken as persons are moved to witness, pray, or sing. There may be response to the sermon on the part of one or more "reactors" or an open "talk-back" session. Local traditions and the character of the proclamation that has just taken place will determine what is appropriate. Or a hymn may be sung.

3) Baptism, confirmation, profession or renewal of faith, reception into membership by transfer, recognitions, dedications, or other special communal acts. (See "A Service of Baptism, Confirmation, and Renewal," *We Gather Together,* pp. 13-17).

4) An affirmation of faith. When *A Service of Baptism, Confirmation, and Renewal* is used, it is appropriate that all those present be invited to reaffirm their faith. On Sundays when this rite is not used, the affirmation of faith serves to remind us of our baptism and the faith in which we were baptized. The affirmation is appropriate either immediately following the sermon or following any of the other responses listed above.

5) Confession/pardon sequence. This has more commonly been done as part of the opening prayers, as was described above, but it often functions better here. Whether or not this is appropriate will depend in large measure on the type of sermon that has just been preached. The confession/pardon sequence may be followed immediately by exchanging the peace, or by concerns and prayers, concluding with the peace.

Concerns and Prayers

This has been known by some United Methodists as the pastoral prayer, but the phrase "concerns and prayers" better indicates that the whole church family is at prayer. Here are some other possible forms:

1) Persons in the congregation may express concerns and prayer requests and pray spontaneously.

2) Persons in the congregation may express concerns and prayer requests, after which the leader prays or leads a directed prayer. In some situations the concerns expressed may call for a specific commitment to an act of service.

3) Persons in the congregation may pass request cards forward, or prior to the service may make the leader aware of their concerns. The leader may or may not announce these concerns before praying. With these concerns and requests in mind, a pastoral prayer or a directed prayer is used.

4) Prayers for the congregation and for the world are gathered into a litany and prayed responsively by the pastor (or other leader) and people. Congregations may also participate in litanies without a printed text in front of them by praying a simple response after each petition.

The size and character of the congregation and of the space in which they worship will help to indicate which of these forms is most practicable and effective.

It is crucial that these be the prayers of the congregation, whether expressed directly by the people or indirectly through the leader, and that they be seen and experienced as such by the people. This is a time for prayers that are as specific as possible—intercessions for persons or causes, petitions for particular needs, and thanksgivings for recent blessings. These concerns and prayers are responses to the Word and part of the people's offerings. These acts connect prayer and Christian action in the world.

The Peace

Scripture teaches that if we are about to offer our gift and there remember that someone has something against us, we should leave our gift and go at once to make peace with that person, then come back and offer our gift (Matt. 5:23-24).

Immediately before the offering many congregations offer one another signs of reconciliation and love by exchanging gestures and words of God's peace, remembering that Christ invites to his table all who love him and desire to live in peace with one another, within and beyond this community. It is a way of acting out the words of the familiar invitation: "Ye that do truly and earnestly repent of your sins, and are in love and charity with your neighbors. . . . " It is an ancient gesture of sealing the prayers that have gone before with a "kiss of peace" as well as a preparation for the Lord's table.

As noted above, this act may also follow the confession/pardon sequence.

The peace is an essential act in the Lord's Supper, which may vary widely, both in character and expression, depending on the character of the congregation and the nature of the occasion. For some, it will be a gesture primarily of love, for others primarily of reconciliation. Depending on the seating arrangement and the degree of intimacy perceived as authentic for the people, this act may consist in a simple handshake, a clasping of both hands, an embrace, or a kiss. The words may be elaborate: "the peace of the Lord be with you." "And also with you." They may also be simple: "Peace." "Amen." They may also be spontaneous, as individuals are moved. Intensity and significance may vary from time to time, and genuine differences of temperament and conviction should be respected.

Offering

The offering is more than money; it is the symbolic offering to God of ourselves and all that we have. It is the corporate self-giving of God's people, in the spirit of

Romans 12:1, "Offer yourselves as a living sacrifice to God, dedicated to his service and pleasing to him" (TEV). This is the mystery of giving back to God the gifts of his creation, including signs of our labor, so that we know that all we have and are is a trust from God. While the offering is being received, there may be instrumental or choral music or congregational singing. When the offering is brought forward and laid on the Lord's table, it is fitting that the congregation stand. A doxology or some other appropriate stanza may be sung.

Taking the Bread and Cup

This is the first of the four basic actions of the Lord's Supper. These are based on the New Testament accounts of what Jesus himself did. He took bread, gave thanks, broke it, and gave it to his disciples. After the supper in the upper room, he took the cup, gave thanks, and gave it to his disciples. Therefore, (1) as Jesus took the bread and the cup, so do we; (2) as Jesus gave thanks over the bread and cup, so do we; (3) as Jesus broke the bread, so do we; and (4) as Jesus gave the bread and cup to his disciples, so we give them to one another.

It is evident that the Lord's Supper is far more than words. Indeed, in our celebrations the verbal is often overdone and the four basic actions neglected. Only the second of these is primarily verbal; the other three are primarily nonverbal acts.

The bread and wine may be presented in various ways. Some congregations bring forward the Communion elements with, or immediately following, the money offering. This may be done by those who have prepared the elements or by other persons from the congregation. In some congregations all the people come forward past the Lord's table to present their offerings, and the presentation of the elements may be inluded in this action. In some congregations the elements are already on the table and covered during the first part of the service and are uncovered during or immediately following the offering.

After taking or uncovering the elements, the minister does any necessary preparation of the bread and wine. More and more congregations find that a large uncut loaf of bread is symbolically more powerful than small cubes or wafers that are invisible to most of the people. The symbol of a chalice is also powerful, even if the people are to be drinking from individual cups. The bread should not be broken at this time, but if the wine is in a flagon or cruet some of it may be poured into the cup at this time. For Holy Communion, the use of food and drink that looks, feels, tasts, and smells like real food and drink can deepen our awareness of the relationships between God's gifts of creation and redemption.

This whole action is nonverbal. It may be done in complete silence. No prayer is necessary before the offering or as the money and the bread and wine are being presented since the Great Thanksgiving that is to follow includes everything that needs to be said at this time.

The Great Thanksgiving

The Great Thanksgiving includes what had formerly been considered several separate prayers, chiefly the prayer of consecration. There was one great prayer of thanksgiving in the early church, but in the Middle Ages this simplicity and unity were lost and are only now being recovered in our tradition and in the ecumenical church.

This great prayer is a Christian version of the type of table blessing which Jesus undoubtedly used. In the New Testament the verb "blessed" is used interchangeably with "give thanks." In ancient Hebrew tradition, the food and drink are blessed by blessing the name of God and recalling his mighty acts. The Great Thanksgiving likewise recalls God's acts from a Christian perspective. It blesses God for the gifts of his creation and redemption, tells the meaning of our actions at the Lord's table, and invokes the power of the Holy Spirit. By ancient tradition it concludes with the Lord's Prayer, which should be prayed in unison. It is the very heartbeat of what we proclaim and live as a community of the creation, crucifixion, and resurrection, who know the presence of the living Christ and look for his final victory. Because of the central importance of thanksgiving in the Lord's Supper, the whole service has historically been called the Eucharist, which is the New Testament word for "thanksgiving."

While this prayer is to be led by a minister authorized to administer the Lord's Supper, congregational participation is also provided for. The responses should be said by the entire congregation or sung by the entire congregation. A musical setting of *The Sacrament of the Lord's Supper: An Alternate Text* has been published, and other settings are found in *The Book of Hymns*.

The ancient custom is for the congregation to stand for the entire prayer and for the minister(s) to stand behind the table, if possible, and face the congregatiion. If the congregation are not already standing, they should be invited to stand before the opening dialogue of the Great Thanksgiving.

Where circumstances permit, especially in smaller services, the whole congregation may come forward from where they been seated and stand around the Lord's table for the Lord's Supper. The taking of the bread and cup is an appropriate time for this coming forward to take place, but it might also take place at the invitation to Christian discipleship or immediately before the people receive Communion.

A variety of alternate texts for the Great Thanksgiving is

found in *At the Lord's Table* (SWR 9). These may be used with the people's parts on page 9 of this volume or page 3 of *We Gather Together* (SWR 10).

Breaking the Bread

The breaking of bread is a gesture of invitation done in the name of the living Christ, the Head of his family and the Host at this meal. It can be done in such a way that persons immediately perceive its meaning, as when the minister, standing behind the Lord's table, lifts the unbroken loaf and in view of the people breaks it by hand. Even if individual wafers or pieces of bread are used, a large wafer or piece of bread or a symbolic loaf should be broken. When the minister cannot stand behind the table, the bread can at least be broken where the action can be seen by the people and perceived as a sign of invitation. After the bread has been broken, it is a natural gesture of invitation to raise the cup before the people.

These acts may be done in silence, or appropriate words may be spoken. Such words express a part, but only a part, of the rich symbolism of these gestures. Our unity in Christ, the message of distributive justice (bread for the world), the breaking of Jesus' body on the cross and the pouring out of his blood, and the Emmaus appearance when the risen Christ was recoognized in "the breaking of the bread"— these are but a few of the possible meanings.

Giving the Bread and Cup

The giving of the bread and wine has traditionally been called the Communion. The word "communion" is a translation of the Greek word *koinonia* in I Corinthians 10:16-17, which can also be translated "participation."

"fellowship," or "sharing." Each of these translations adds a new dimension to the meaning of *koinonia*.

This sharing is, of course, primarily nonverbal, but words are usually exchanged as the bread and cup are given and received. The congregation may sing during the Communion, thus reinforcing the communal nature of the celebration. Opportunity may be given for spontaneous song and praise.

The giving and receiving of the bread and cup can be done in various ways, depending on the size of the congregation and the design of the space in which they are worshiping.

Many congregations are accustomed to going forward in groups, kneeling at the rail in groups, receiving the bread and cup from the hands of the minister, and then being dismissed in groups. While many persons find this style meaningful, it can become an almost unbearably lengthy process when the congregation is large. To reduce the amount of time involved, additional ministers or lay persons can assist behind the rail in the serving of the bread and cup, and persons may come and go freely at the rail rather than by "tables."

Many other congregations pass the bread and cup from hand to hand where they are seated. This has the advantage of taking less time, but the disadvantage that the people are denied the opportunity to be active—to move forward rather than sit passively and wait. Where this pattern is followed, the people should be encouraged to make the serving of the persons next to them a personal gesture of sharing, perhaps spontaneously exchanging appropriate words. It is not necessary that all the people wait to eat or drink together at the same time.

An increasing number of congregations are finding that going forward, moving continuously past one or more places where the bread and cup are being given, and receiving Communion standing combines advantages of receiving kneeling or seated.

At services where the congregation can stand gathered around the Lord's table the people can easily and informally serve one another, with words as the Spirit moves.

However the elements are distributed, two things should be clear. One is that the invitation is extended to all those present. The other is that persons who prefer not to receive the bread and wine should be able to refrain without embarrassment.

In any case, this giving and receiving should be a clear and powerful acting out of the gospel. It is God's giving of himself to us through another person. For this reason, one person should serve another. Therefore, "self-service" Communion, where persons go to the table or to the rail and help themselves to the elements, should not be practiced, since it destroys the symbolism and power of the giving and receiving. Likewise, the practice of having the place of worship open over a period of time for persons to enter and leave as they wish, to take the elements without participating in the prayer and praise of the church, destroys the communal nature of the service and therefore is strongly discouraged.

When all have received the bread and cup, the remaining elements are returned to the table, and it is set in order.

Here the symbolic power of what we do with the remaining elements should not be underestimated. They may be set aside for distribution to the sick and others wishing Communion but unable to attend. They may be respectfully consumed by the ministers and others while the table is being put in order or following the service. They may be returned to the earth—a biblical gesture of worship (see II Sam. 23:16) and an ecological symbol today. Whatever we choose to do should express our stewardship of God's gifts and our respect for the purpose which these elements have served.

41

[Closing Prayer]

We have come to the end of the four basic actions at the Lord's table, but many wish to pause at this point for a brief prayer thanking God for enabling us to share this meal in the Spirit and expressing the connection between our having received and our being sent to serve others in God's name.

Hymn or Song

A final hymn or song seems just as fitting as an opening hymn or song. If it is a recessional in which the minister joins, it should follow the dismissal with blessing. Many congregations sing a favorite hymn, song, stanza, or doxology at this point in every service. If the congregation has been singing during the giving of the bread and cup and if there is no closing prayer, this may simply be the last of the hymns or songs sung. In some circumstances spontaneous song or spoken praise is appropriate.

Dismissal with Blessing

This final act may consist of two parts: the dismissal, which sends us from our corporate worship into the wider world to serve in God's name, and the blessing, which is pronounced in the name of God by the minister to the people, face to face.

Going Forth

The church now scatters to continue its service of God in the life of the world. Like the gathering, this too is an act of worship and not simply necessary mechanics.

When the Lord's Supper Is Not Celebrated (Non-Communion Days)

On days when the Lord's Supper is not celebrated the service may still incorporate the elements of the peace, offering, thanksgiving, and sharing that are more fully expressed in the Lord's Supper.

There are several places in the service where the sharing of the peace may be appropriate, as well as before the offering. It may follow the opening prayer(s), or it may follow the response to the Word, especially if either of these has included a confession/pardon sequence.

The offering follows the concerns and prayers and can have the same significance that it has when the Lord's Supper is celebrated, except that there is no bread and wine to bring forward or uncover.

A prayer of thanksgiving follows the offering, in the place of the Great Thanksgiving. The thanksgiving is not for the money, but rather it should be focused upon God's reality. It is not a blessing of the money but a blessing of God. In this sense, it should reflect the Great Thanksgiving over the bread and cup and should anticipate the next celebration of the Lord's Supper. The Lord's Prayer is a fitting act of unison prayer at the conclusion of this thanksgiving, as at the conclusion of the Great Thanksgiving.

The service concludes with a final hymn, song, stanza, doxology, or instrumental music and the dismissal with blessing. The sharing of signs and words of fellowship following the dismissal with blessing is already customary in most United Methodist congregations and reflects the spirit of the peace. This sharing is an echo and an anticipation of the sharing of the bread and cup at the Lord's Supper.

IV.
The Ecumenical Calendar and Lectionary

Thus far we have dealt with the structure and many items which remain constant from Sunday to Sunday. But Christian worship is also a mixture of items that change from week to week. Chief among these are the scripture lessons, psalms, hymns, sermon, and (perhaps) opening prayer. These give variety to Christian worship while the unchanging items give it stability. Readers of this volume are urged to consult *Seasons of the Gospel* (SWR 6), which treats the variable elements of worship in detail and contains the new ecumenical lectionary in a United Methodist version. These resources are arranged on the basis of the Christian year as structured in the calendar found on page 11 of this volume.

The Christian year begins the First Sunday in Advent, which is the Fourth Sunday before Christmas and always falls during the period November 27 through December 3. By ecumenical agreement, Year A in the three-year lectionary cycle begins the First Sunday in Advent 1980, 1983, 1986, etc. Year B begins the First Sunday in Advent, 1981, 1984, 1987, etc. Year C begins the First Sunday in Advent, 1982, 1985, 1988, etc.

Three Scripture lections are suggested for each Sunday. This opens up various possibilities. All three lections may be read each Sunday. The sermon may relate these Scriptures to each other and to present-day life. This is, however, more readily done on some days than on others; and the sermon may center upon one or two of the Scriptures. The preacher who uses only one Scripture can thereby turn the three-year cycle into a nine-year cycle. The pastor who preaches twice on Sundays and perhaps in the middle of the week has the basis for two or three sermons a week in this lectionary. In no way is this lectionary intended to take from preachers their right to use their judgment as to the Scriptures and sermons needed by a particular congregation at a particular time.

There are, however, some real advantages in using the lectionary week after week. The lectionary helps ministers, musicians, and other involved persons to plan ahead and work with one another. Because the lectionary covers the Bible in a systematic and balanced way, a minister by reading and preaching from the suggested Scriptures over a three-year period will have dealt with all the great themes of the Bible. The minister who has a tendency to preach only from certain parts of the Bible and ignore other parts will find lectionary preaching a good discipline. Preachers who follow the lectionary report that it is amazing how relevant the suggested lections can be. The lectionary is intended not to restrict but to set free, not to close off other options but to broaden horizons and open up new options.

There are even wider uses to which the lectionary can be put. A church school class or a midweek Bible study group can study these lections, either before or after the worship service at which these Scriptures are read and preached. The congregation, and especially the minister, can be encouraged to use these passages in their daily devotions during the preceding week. Such practices reinforce the impact of these Scriptures in a congregation.

A wide variety of worship, preaching, and study resources is now being published, based on this lectionary. One of the great advantages of a lectionary that is common to many denominations is the way in which it facilitates the publication and sale of such resources.[1]

Since the ecumenical lectionary confines itself to generally observed days and seasons, distinctively United Methodist and civil observances are not included; but a United Methodist pastor and congregation can easily include these observances while using this lectionary.

Kingdomtide, for instance, can be observed by any church that wishes to do so by simply changing the seasonal color on the last Sunday in August and listing the Sundays from then through the fall as First Sunday in Kingdomtide, etc., while choosing the Scriptures from the lectionary according to the numbered Sundays after Pentecost. The suggested lections are quite suitable for a Kingdomtide emphasis.

Various special days are promoted by our denominational agencies, and these agencies sometimes suggest Scripture readings that can be used in place of the lectionary Scriptures if desired. Other special days are observed by local and national custom. Many ministers prefer to use the lectionary and take note of these special days in other ways. The lectionary in *The Book of Hymns* and *The Book of Worship* has a section on special days, which can be followed by anyone who wishes to use these resources.

On the other hand, it is important that the calendar not be seen as a collection of special days but as a Christ-centered whole, repeatedly reminding us of events in the saving work of Christ. We are pressed to make up our minds what we really believe about Jesus Christ.

Advent, for instance, focuses our attention on the past, present, and future comings of Christ so that we, too, may

46

be a people prepared for his coming. We need no urging to celebrate Christmas, but why do our celebrations so often stop short the next day? The Epiphany is an older, and possibly even more profound, commemoration than Christmas and stresses the mystery of the manifestation of God in Jesus Christ. The visit of the wise men, the baptism of the Lord, and the Transfiguration all deal with miraculous epiphanies.

Lent was originally the final period of preparation for those who were to be baptized at Easter and also the time when those already baptized examined anew what it meant to be a Christian in preparation for the renewal of their baptismal covenant at Easter. Lent can still have this meaning for us today. Holy week, the climax of Lent, begins with Palm/Passion Sunday. It may seem strange that Palm Sunday is also Passion Sunday, but it makes excellent sense if we are to confront congregations today with what it means to be a follower of Christ. Most persons who worship on Palm Sunday and Easter do not attend the weekday services in between. To pass directly from the lesser triumph of the entry into Jerusalem to the greater triumph of the Resurrection without coming to terms with the passion that came between these two events would be to distort the gospel. Ways of combining the Palm and Passion emphases in one service are fully described in *From Ashes to Fire: Services of Worship for the Seasons of Lent and Easter with Introduction and Commentary* (SWR 8), pages 50-95.

Easter is more than a single hour of celebration. We will expand our understanding of death and resurrection through the observance of the Easter Vigil, on Easter Eve or at Easter sunrise. This very ancient Christian celebration, with all its Scriptures, has such great potential as the very climax of the Christian year that we are planning later to offer additional resources for its recovery and celebration.

The note of resurrection victory should pervade worship and proclamation throughout the Easter season.

Ascension, originally a part of Pentecost, raises questions about the close of Jesus' historical visibility and the continuance of his work—questions to which a tremendous affirmative answer is given on Pentecost. Later in the year All Saints' Day, the annual Christian memorial service, stresses the same point: how Christ continues to work through time and space.

The Christian year comes to a triumphant close on the theme of Christ the King. Where the season of Kingdomtide is observed, it points to God's ultimate victory and reign through Jesus Christ. In any case, the lections on the Last Sunday after Pentecost (or the Last Sunday in Kingdomtide) proclaim the kingship of Christ. This celebration is the crown that closes the Christian year. It also leads immediately into the beginning of the new Christian year as Advent begins the following Sunday. Thus expectation gives way to Advent as year suceeds year.

Since ancient times Christian have divided the year into these days and seasons of special Christian significance.[2] This "sanctification of time" that we call the Christian year—or the church year or the calendar—not only gives Christian meaning to the days and seasons of the year but also is a way of encouraging, over a period of time, a balanced presentation of the various events in the history of salvation and the various emphases of Christian teaching. Through the centuries, while there has been much denominational variation in the observance of the Christian year, in essentials it is a unifying heritage.

In recent years Christians have been cooperating more closely with one another in many areas of ministry and mission, not the least of which have been the observances of the Christian year. *The Book of Worship* (1965) and *The Book of Hymns (The Methodist Hymnal,* 1966) marked for our denomination a great advance in the presentation and observance of the Christian year and were based upon what had taken place in other Christian denominations. Since these books were published, much further development of the Christian year has taken place among Roman Catholic, Episcopal, Lutheran, Presbyterian, Christian Church (Disciples of Christ), and United Church of Christ denominations.

Closely related to the calendar of the Christian year is the lectionary, which is a cycle of Scripture readings for each Sunday and other major days of the Christian year. This, too, has existed since ancient times, with denominational variations. Some denominations, such as the Episcopal and Lutheran, tended to follow more closely the traditional Roman Catholic lectionary. Other lectionaries, such as the one in *The Book of Worship* and *The Book of Hymns,* have much less in common with that ancient lectionary but were attempts to develop a realistic modern lectionary and represented great steps forward for the denominations involved. A monumental comparison of these ancient and modern lectionaries was made by William F. Dunkle, Jr., and published as chapter 8 of *Companion to the Book of Worship.*[3]

In 1963 the Roman Catholic Church at Vatican Council II decided that in worship "the treasures of the Bible should be opened up more lavishly so that richer fare might be provided for the faithful at the table of God's Word. In this way a more representative portion of sacred Scripture will be read to the people over a set cycle of years." (*Constitution on the Sacred Liturgy,* Article 51) This decision led to six years of compressed biblical and lectionary studies, experimentation, and revisions with a thoroughness unequalled in the history of the church. During these years the Consilium for the Implementation of the Constitution on the Sacred Liturgy sought and heeded the advice of hundreds of biblical and liturgical experts from the whole range of Christian denominations, including United Methodists. This effort bore fruit at the beginning of the 1970 Christian year, when the new lectionary was put into effect for the Roman Catholic Church. Whereas the historic Catholic lectionary and most modern lectionaries had been based on a one-year cycle, the new lectionary was based on a three-year cycle. Where the traditional lectionary had two readings each Sunday, the new lectionary had three. As a result, the new lectionary had a far greater coverage of the Bible than older lectionaries and was soon widely acknowledged by scholars and worship leaders of many denominations as the most carefully prepared, most comprehensive, and probably finest lectionary in Christian history.

This new lectionary immediately caught the interest of American Protestants. Many of them had been consulted in its prepartion and were impressed with it.

Since the Episcopal Church was in the process of revising *The Book of Common Prayer*, it was natural that it should consider, revise, and then adopt the new Roman Catholic lectionary. Several hundred consultants, both in and outside of the Episcopal denominations, were consulted during the revision stage. In that process, a number of changes were made in the calendar and lections. The resulting lectionary went into trial use among Episcopalians in 1970. A further revision was made in October 1973, and was finally approved in September 1979.

In the fall of 1970 the Joint Committee on Worship for the Cumberland Presbyterian Church, the Presbyterian Church in the United States, and the United Presbyterian Church in the United States of America published *The Worshipbook*, containing still another version of this lectionary. Though following the basic pattern, it contained numerous changes, especially regarding the verses at which the lections began and ended. It was later included in *The Hymnal of the United Church of Christ* (1974) and recommended by the Christian Church (Disciples of Christ).

In 1973 the Inter-Lutheran Commission on Worship, representing the Lutheran Church in America, the American Lutheran Church, the Evangelical Lutheran Church of Canada, and the Lutheran Church—Missouri Synod, published yet another version of this lectionary. This finally appeared in the 1978 *Lutheran Book of Worship.*

In the fall of 1972 the Commission on Worship of the Consultation on Church Union (COCU), meeting in Washington, D. C., began work on a lectionary, both as a means of contributing to church unity and as a service to those churches which did not have a recent lectionary.

It soon became apparent that a calendar must first be prepared. This was done and adopted at the commission's meeting in Chicago in February 1973. At that time it was decided to omit national and civic holidays from the calendar, because of wide diversity in the uses of the various denominations with respect to such days. It was recognized that there are also distinctively denominational observances. Churches and denominations were, of course, free to choose their own additional days and lections.

With the calendar decided upon, work continued on the lectionary.

It was decided that the eighteen readings from the Apocryphal books (which appear in the Roman Catholic and Episcopal lectionaries) were to be listed separately for optional use. This was deemed necessary since many current pulpit Bibles do not include these books.

The drafting of the lectionary was done by James F. White, assisted by Hoyt Hickman, both United Mehodists, and under the guidance of the commission.

They worked from a collation of the Roman Catholic, Episcopal, Presbyterian, and Lutheran lectionaries, arranged in parallel columns. The Episcopal column was revised to include the changes made by the denomination late in 1973.

The basic objective was to create a consensus lectionary as much as possible. When three sources agreed, that choice was taken. When two agreed and not the others, then the two agreeing provided the obvious choice. When no two agreed, decisions had to be made as to which lection best fitted the sequence. No lection was introduced that was not already in one or more of the four existing versions. An effort was made to include the longest version of each lection, with the expectation that those reading the lections in worship might choose to abbreviate but were less likely to expand a reading, and with the hope that this method of inclusiveness would be useful in the study of the text.

A preliminary draft of the resulting COCU lectionary was approved in principle at the October 1973 meeting of the COCU Commission on Worship and was used experimentally in some local churches for the next few months.

An index was then prepared, and it became apparent that choosing from differing lectionaries had caused a number of lections to be repeated. These duplications were largely eliminated except where all four lectionaries included repetitions.[4]

Final approval was then given to the lectionary by COCU, and it was published by the commission under the title *A Lectionary* in October 1974.

Meanwhile, the Section on Worship of the United Methodist Board of Discipleship, at their October 1973 meeting, had set up a task force under the leadership of Don Saliers to prepare resources for weekly worship, including a calendar and lectionary, as part of the Alternate Rituals Project. This task force was aware of the work being done on a COCU calendar and lectionary, and they quickly agreed to work together with COCU on the project, designating James F. White and Hoyt Hickman as their subcommittee on the calendar and lectionary. During the following months of joint testing and revision of the preliminary COCU draft, it as evident that there was no reason for the United Methodist alternate calendar and lectionary to be other than the COCU calendar and lectionary, except for the addition of the special days from the lectionary in *The Book of Hymns* and *The Book of Worship* that were not in the COCU calendar and lectionary.

Then the Section on Worship met in October 1974 and examined *A Lectionary,* which had been published by COCU only a few days before. They recommended that, with the addition of the above-mentioned special days and with an appropriately revised preface, the COCU calendar and lectionary be included in the forthcoming resources published in the Supplemental Worship Resources. Until this could be done, *A Lectionary* was recommended for study and optional use by United Methodists. In the months that followed, several thousand United Methodists requested and received copies of *A Lectionary;* and their response to it was overwhelmingly favorable. The final decision to include this calendar and lectionary in the book was made by the Section on Worship at its October 1975 meeting.

At this meeting the hope was expressed that Psalter could be included with the lectionary when it was published and that the cooperation of COCU be sought toward this end. This was reported a few days later to the Steering Committee of the COCU Worship Commission, and they authorized Hoyt Hickman, in consultation with James F. White, to draw up a consensus Psalter on the same principles that were followed in the drawing up of the lectionary.

With the Psalter there were only three comparable versions to be considered, all following the three-year cycle of the lectionary and closely parallel to one another: the

Roman Catholic, the Episcopal, and the Lutheran. These three Psalters were arranged in parallel columns, and a consensus Psalter was drawn up. Where all versions agreed, the choice was obvious. Where two versions agreed, the selection on which they agreed was chosen except in a few instances where there were strong reasons for choosing the other selection. When there was no agreement, or in other difficult cases, the Psalter passages in question were examined, together with the first lections recommended to precede them in each of the three lectionaries and the COCU lectionary. Often different Psalter selections were found to reflect different first lections, and the choice as normally made to follow those whose first lections corresponded with ours. An index was prepared,[5] and care was taken not to repeat a psalm more often than clear ecumenical consensus would justify.

This consensus Psalter was submitted to the COCU Worship Commission meeting in February 1976. The Commission was not in a position to act as quickly as the United Methodists on the Psalter, but they saw no difficulty in the United Methodists' publishing the Psalter on their own.

Later that month this Psalter was approved for publication by the Executive Editorial Committee of the Section on Worship. Approved with it was a second Psalter, which had not been submitted to COCU but which used the Psalter in *The Book of Hymns* in a one-year cycle.

Subsequent refinements in the calendar and lectionary have been incorporated into the calendar on page 11 of this volume and the lectionary in *Seasons of the Gospel* (SWR 6), where the history and reasoning behind these recent refinements is given on pages 44-46.

V.
Ecumenical Texts

The following ancient and biblical worship texts have long been used by Christians of many denominations, but in a variety of slightly differing English translations. In 1969 the International Consultation on English Texts was set up, representing all major English-speaking countries and denominations using these acts of worship, to develop English translations that might be used by Christians of any denomination or nation. Preliminary translations were published for trial use in 1970 and 1971, and in 1975 the final texts were published with a foreword and commentary under the title *Prayers We Have in Common*[6] from which the texts below are taken.

Kyrie

Kyrie eleison.	Lord, have mercy.
Christe eleison.	Christ, have mercy.
Kyrie eleison.	Lord, have mercy.

Gloria in Excelsis

Glory to God in the highest,
    and peace to his people on earth.

Lord God, heavenly King,
almighty God and Father,
  we worship you, we give you thanks,
  we praise you for your glory.

Lord Jesus Christ, only Son of the Father,
Lord God, Lamb of God,
you take away the sin of the World:
  have mercy on us;
you are seated at the right hand of the Father:
  receive our prayer.

For you alone are the Holy One,
you alone are the Lord,
you alone are the Most High,
  Jesus Christ,
  with the Holy Spirit,
  in the glory of God the Father. Amen.

Gloria Patri

Glory to the Father, and to the Son, and to the Holy Spirit: as
  it was in the beginning, is now, and will be forever.
  Amen.

The Apostles' Creed

I believe in God, the Father almighty,
  creator of heaven and earth.

I believe in Jesus Christ, his only Son, our Lord.
  He was conceived by the power of the Holy Spirit
    and born of the Virgin Mary.
  He suffered under Pontius Pilate,
    was crucified, died, and was buried.

He descended to the dead.
On the third day he rose again.
He ascended into heaven,
    and is seated at the right hand of the Father.
He will come again to judge the living and the dead.

I believe in the Holy Spirit,
    the holy catholic Church,
    the communion of saints,
    the forgiveness of sins,
    the resurrection of the body
    and the life everlasting. Amen.

The Nicene Creed

We believe in one God,
    the Father, the Almighty,
    maker of heaven and earth,
    of all that is, seen and unseen.

We believe in one Lord, Jesus Christ,
    the only Son of God,
    eternally begotten of the Father,
    God from God, Light from Light,
    true God from true God,
    begotten, not made,
    of one Being with the Father.
    Through him all things were made.
    For us and for our salvation
        he came down from heaven:
    by the power of the Holy Spirit
        he became incarnate from the Virgin Mary,
        and was made man.
    For our sake he was crucified under Pontius Pilate;
        he suffered death and was buried.
        On the third day he rose again
            in accordance with the Scriptures;

he ascended into heaven
and is seated at the right hand of the Father.
He will come again in glory
to judge the living and the dead,
and his kingdom will have no end.

We believe in the Holy Spirit, the Lord, the giver of life,
who proceeds from the Father and the Son.
With the Father and the Son
he is worshiped and glorified.
He has spoken through the Prophets.
We believe in one holy catholic and apostolic Church.
We acknowledge one baptism
for the forgiveness of sins.
We look for the resurrection of the dead,
and the life of the world to come. Amen.

Sursum Corda

The Lord be with you.

And also with you.

Lift up your hearts.

We lift them to the Lord.

Let us give thanks to the Lord our God.

It is right to give him thanks and praise.

Sanctus and Benedictus

Holy, holy, holy Lord, God of power and might,
heaven and earth are full of your glory.
Hosanna in the highest.
Blessed is he who comes in the name of the Lord.
Hosanna in the highest.

The Lord's Prayer

Our Father in heaven,
  hallowed be your Name,
  your kingdom come,
  your will be done,
    on earth as in heaven.
Give us today our daily bread.
Forgive us our sins
  as we forgive those who sin against us.
Save us from the time of trial
  and deliver us from evil.
For the kingdom, the power, and the glory are yours
  now and for ever.

Agnus Dei

Jesus, Lamb of God:
  have mercy on us.
Jesus, bearer of our sins:
  have mercy on us.
Jesus, redeemer of the world;
  give us your peace.

Benedictus—
The Song of Zechariah—Luke 1:68-79

Blessed be the Lord, the God of Israel;
he has come to his people and set them free.
He has raised up for us a mighty savior,
born of the house of his servant David.
Through his holy prophets he promised of old
  that he would save us from our enemies,
  from the hands of all who hate us.

He promised to show mercy to our fathers
and to remember his holy covenant.
This was the oath he swore to our father Abraham:
to set us free from the hands of our enemies,
free to worship him without fear,
holy and righteous in his sight
  all the days of our life.

You, my child, shall be called the prophet of the Most
    High,
for you will go before the Lord to prepare his way
to give his people knowledge of salvation
by the forgiveness of their sins.
In the tender compassion of our God
the dawn from on high shall break upon us,
to shine on those who dwell in darkness
  and the shadow of death,
and to guide our feet into the way of peace.

Te Deum

You are God: we praise you;
you are the Lord: we acclaim you:
You are the eternal Father:
All creation worships you.
To you all angels, all the powers of heaven,
Cherubim and Seraphim, sing in endless praise:
  Holy, holy, holy Lord, God of power and might,
  heaven and earth are full of your glory.
The glorious company of apostles praise you.
The noble fellowship of prophets praise you.
The white-robed army of martyrs praise you.
Throughout the world the holy Church acclaims you:
  Father, of majesty unbounded,
  your true and only Son, worthy of all worship,
  and the Holy Spirit, advocate and guide.

You, Christ, are the King of glory,
the eternal Son of the Father.
When you become man to set us free
you did not spurn the Virgin's womb.
You overcame the sting of death,
and opened the kingdom of heaven to all believers.
You are seated at God's right hand in glory.
We believe that you will come, and be our judge.
   Come then, Lord, and help your people,
   bought with the price of your own blood,
   and bring us with your saints
   to glory everlasting.

Versicles and Responses
After the Te Deum

Save your people, Lord, and bless your inheritance.
Govern and uphold them now and always.
Day by day we bless you.
We praise your name for ever.
Keep us today, Lord, from all sin.
Have mercy on us, Lord, have mercy.
Lord, show us your love and mercy;
for we put our trust in you.
In you, Lord, is our hope:
and we shall never hope in vain.

Magnificat—
The Song of Mary—Luke 1:46-55

My soul proclaims the greatness of the Lord,
my spirit rejoices in God my Savior;
for he has looked with favor on his lowly servant.
From this day all generations will call me blessed:

61

the Almighty has done great things for me,
and holy is his Name.
He has mercy on those who fear him
in every generation.
He has shown the strength of his arm,
he has scattered the proud in their conceit.
He has cast down the mighty from their thrones,
and has lifted up the lowly.
He has filled the hungry with good things,
and the rich he has sent away empty.
He has come to the help of his servant Israel
for he has remembered his promise of mercy,
the promise he made to our fathers,
to Abraham and his children for ever.

Nunc Dimittis—
*The Song of Simeon—*Luke 2:29-32

Lord, now you let your servant go in peace;
your word has been fulfilled:
my own eyes have seen the salvation
which you have prepared in the sight of every people:
a light to reveal you to the nations
and the glory of your people Israel.

VI.
List of Committee Members

Section on Worship of the Board of Discipleship

Eugene C. Holmes, Chairperson, Section on Worship
H. Grady Hardin, Chairperson, Editorial Committee
Rosalie Bentzinger
Phyllis Close
Grace Etcheto
L. L. Haynes, Jr.
Patti Russell
Robert Scoggin
Louise Shown
Laurence H. Stookey
Bishop John Warman
Roberto Escamilla, Assistant General Secretary
Hoyt Hickman, Staff
Thom Jones, Staff

Task Force on Word and Table
Don E Saliers, Chairperson
Julian Hartt
James F. White
Hoyt Hickman, Staff

Notes

1. For an up-to-date listing of these lectionary-based resources, write the Section on Worship, P. O. Box 840, Nashville, Tennessee 37202.
2. Much of this history is adapted with permission from the preface to *A Lectionary*, pp. 1-7, available from COCU, 228 Alexander St., Princeton, N.J. 08540.
3. Edited by William F. Dunkle, Jr. and Joseph D. Quillan, Jr. (Nashville: Abingdon Press, 1970).
4. An index of the lections in their biblical order is contained in *Seasons of the Gospel* (Nashville: Abingdon, 1979), pp. 115-30.
5. Cf. *Seasons of the Gospel.* pp. 130-33.
6. International Consultation on English Texts (Philadelphia; Fortress Press), copyright © 1970, 1971, and 1975.